# MONGOLIAN
# FOR BEGINNERS

## FIRST 1000 WORDS

### EFFIE DELAROSA

# contents

# contents

# contents

| | | |
|---|---|---|
| **Тийм**<br>**[Tijm]**<br><br>Yes | **Үгүй**<br>**[Ügüj]**<br><br>No | **Сайн уу**<br>**[Sajn uu]**<br><br>Hello |
| **Баярлалаа**<br>**[Bajarlalaa]**<br><br>Thank You | **Баяртай**<br>**[Bajartaj]**<br><br>Goodbye | **Тэгэх үү**<br>**[Tègèx üü]**<br><br>Please |
| **ба**<br>**[Ba]**<br>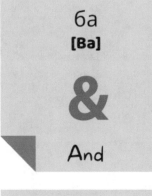<br>And | **Эсвэл**<br>**[Èsvèl]**<br><br>Or | **Энэ**<br>**[Ènè]**<br><br>This |
| **Би**<br>**[Bi]**<br><br>I | **Та**<br>**[Ta]**<br>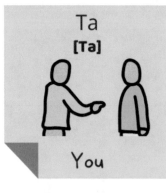<br>You | **Тэр / эрэгтэй**<br>**[Tèr / Èrègtèj]**<br><br>He |
| **Тэр / эмэгтэй**<br>**[Tèr / Èmègtèj]**<br>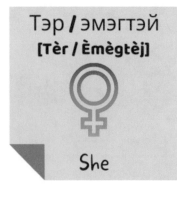<br>She | **Бид**<br>**[Bid]**<br><br>We | **Тэд**<br>**[Tèd]**<br><br>They |

## Уучлаарай
**[Uučlaaraj]**

Sorry

## Гэхдээ
**[Gèxdèè]**

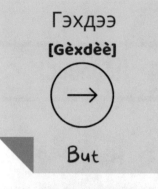

But

## Оройн мэнд
**[Orojn mènd]**

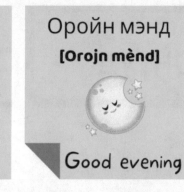

Good evening

## Яагаад гэвэл
**[Jaagaad gèvèl]**

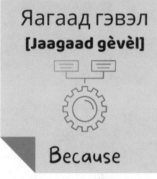

Because

## Тавтай морил
**[Tavtaj moril]**

Welcome

## Хаана
**[Xaana]**

Where

## Юу
**[Juu]**

What

## Хэд вэ
**[Xèd vè]**

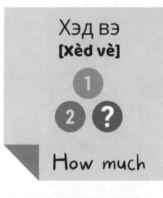

How much

## Аль
**[Al']**

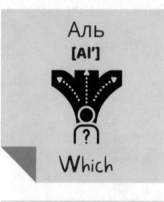

Which

## Гайхалтай
**[Gajxaltaj]**

Awesome

## Хөөрхөн
**[Xöörxön]**

Cute

## Туслалцаа
**[Tuslalcaa]**

Help

## Хэрэв
**[Xèrèv]**

If

## Хэзээ
**[Xèzèè]**

When

## Яагаад
**[Jaagaad]**

Why

# тоонууд

[toonuud]

| | |
|---|---|
| **Тэг** 0 [Tèg] Zero | **Нэг** 1 [Nèg] One |
| **Хоёр** 2 [Xoёr] Two | |

| | |
|---|---|
| **Гурав** 3 [Gurav] Three | **Дөрөв** 4 [Döröv] Four |
| **Тав** 5 [Tav] Five | |

| | |
|---|---|
| **Зургаа** 6 [Zurgaa] Six | **Долоо** 7 [Doloo] Seven |
| **Найм** 8 [Najm] Eight | |

| | |
|---|---|
| **Ес** 9 [Es] Nine | **Арав** 10 [Arav] Ten |
| **Арван тав** 15 [Arvan tav] Fifteen | |

| | |
|---|---|
| **Хорь** 20 [Xor'] Twenty | **Зуу** 100 [Zuu] One Hundred |
| **Мянга** 1000 [Mjanga] One Thousand | |

# ГЭР БҮЛ
## [GÈR BÜL]
### FAMILY

**Ээж**
[Èèž]
Mother

**Аав**
[Aav]
Father

**Ах**
[Ax]
Brother

**Эгч**
[Ègč]
Sister

**Эмээ**
[Èmèè]
Grandmother

**Өвөө**
[Övöö]
Grandfather

**Хүү**
[Xüü]
Son

**Охин**
[Oxin]
Daughter

**Авга/Нагац эгч**
[Avga/Nagac ègč]
Aunt

**Авга/Нагац ах**
[Avga/Nagac ax]
Uncle

**Зээ охин**
[Zèè oxin]
Granddaughter

**Ач хүү**
[Ač xüü]
Grandson

**Эхнэр**
[Èxnèr]
Wife

**Нөхөр**
[Nöxör]
Husband

# Өглөөний цай
[Öglöönij caj]
**Breakfast**

# Үдийн хоол
[Üdijn xool]
**Lunch**

# Оройн хоол
[Orojn xool]
**Dinner**

# Хоол
[Xool]
**Meal**

## Талх
[Talx]
**Bread**

## Бяслаг
[Bjaslag]
**Cheese**

## Өндөг
[Öndög]
**Egg**

## Загас
[Zagas]
**Fish**

## Мах
[Max]
**Meat**

## Масло
[Maslo]
**Butter**

## Хиам
[Xiam]
**Ham**

## Зайдас
[Zajdas]
**Sausage**

## Тараг
[Tarag]
**Yogurt**

## Бялуу
[Bjaluu]
**Cake**

## Шоколад
[Šokolad]
**Chocolate**

# Давс
[Davs]
Salt

# Сахар
[Saxar]
Sugar

# Перец
[Perec]
Pepper

# Уух зүйл
[Uux züjl]
Drink

# Гурил
[Guril]
Flour

# Модтой чихэр
[Modtoj čixèr]
Lollipop

# Зөгийн бал
[Zögijn bal]
Honey

# Донат
[Donat]
Doughnut

# Зайрмаг
[Zajrmag]
Ice Cream

# Ус
[Us]
Water

# Кофе
[Kofe]
Coffee

# Сүү
[Süü]
Milk

# Жүржийн шүүс
[Žüržijn šüüs]
Orange Juice

# Цай
[Caj]
Tea

# Халуун шоколад
[Xaluun šokolad]
Hot Chocolate

# Хоол
[Xool]
Food

# Амин дэм
[Amin dèm]
Vitamin

# Амттан
[Amttan]
Dessert

# Овъёос
[Ov''ёos]
Cereals

# Сонгино
[Songino]
Onion

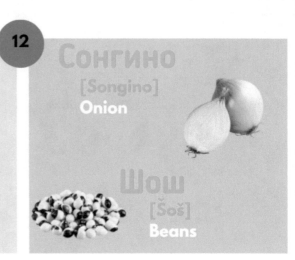

# Шош
[Šoš]
Beans

# Эрдэнэ шиш
[Èrdènè šiš]
Corn

# Улаан буудай
[Ulaan buudaj]
Wheat

# Овъёос
[Ov''ёos]
Oat

# Кетчуп
[Ketčup]
Ketchup

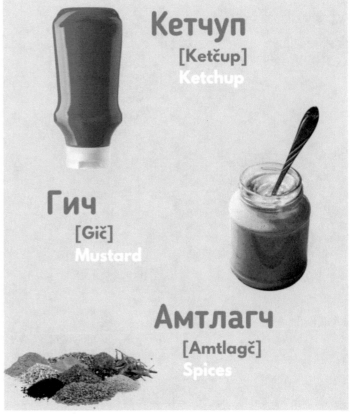

# Гич
[Gič]
Mustard

# Амтлагч
[Amtlagč]
Spices

# Тос
[Tos]
Oil

# Цагаан будаа
[Cagaan budaa]
Rice

# Паста гоймон
[Pasta gojmon]
Pasta

# Тээврийн хэрэгслүүд
## [Tèèvrijn xèrègslüüd]

## vehicles

**Онгоц**
[Ongoc]
AIRPLANE

**Завь**
[Zav']
BOAT

**усан онгоц**
[usan ongoc]
SHIP

**автомашин**
[avtomašin]
CAR

**мотоцикл**
[motocikl]
MOTORBIKE

**галт тэрэг**
[galt tèrèg]
TRAIN

**трактор**
[traktor]
TRACTOR

**унадаг дугуй**
[unadag duguj]
BICYCLE

**автобус**
[avtobus]
BUS

**такси**
[taksi]
TAXI

**метро**
[metro]
SUBWAY

**ачааны машин**
[ačaany mašin]
TRUCK

**түргэн тусламж**
[türgèn tuslamž]
AMBULANCE

**нисдэг тэрэг**
[nisdèg tèrèg]
HELICOPTER

**трамвай**
[tramvaj]
TRAM

# Аялал
## [Ajalal]

travel

**амралт**

[amralt]

**HOLIDAY**

**онгоцны буудал**

[ongocny buudal]

**AIRPORT**

**төмөр замын зогсоол**

[tömör zamyn zogsool]

**TRAIN STATION**

**усан боомт**

[usan boomt]

**PORT**

**жуулчин**

[žuulčin]

**TOURIST**

**зочид буудал**

[zočid buudal]

**HOTEL**

**байшин**

[bajšin]

**HOUSE**

**орон сууц**

[oron suuc]

**APARTMENT**

**чемодан**

[čemodan]

**SUITCASE**

**паспорт**

[pasport]

**PASSPORT**

**газрын зураг**

[gazryn zurag]

**MAP**

**усан сан**

[usan san]

**SWIMMING POOL**

**зам**

[zam]

**ROAD**

**гудамж**

[gudamž]

**STREET**

**явган зам**

[javgan zam]

**WALK**

# Шувуу
## [Šuvuu]
**Bird**

# Муур
## [Muur]
**Cat**

# Нохой
## [Noxoj]
**Dog**

# Нугас
## [Nugas]
**Duck**

# Хулгана
## [Xulgana]
**Mouse**

# Тагтаа
## [Tagtaa]
**Pigeon**

# Туулай
## [Tuulaj]
**Rabbit**

# Заан
## [Zaan]
**Elephant**

# Сармагчин
## [Sarmagčin]
**Monkey**

# Тахиа
## [Taxia]
**Chicken**

# Үнээ
## [Ünèè]
**Cow**

# Илжиг
## [Ilžig]
**Donkey**

# Ямаа
## [Jamaa]
**Goat**

# Морь
## [Moŕ]
**Horse**

# Гахай
## [Gaxaj]
**Pig**

**15**

амьтад

[am'tad]

ANIMALS

## Хонь
### [Xon']

Sheep

## Галуу
### [Galuu]

Goose

## Баавгай
### [Baavgaj]

Bear

## Тэмээ
### [Tèmèè]

Camel

## Мэлхий
### [Mèlxij]

Frog

## Могой
### [Mogoj]

Snake

## Яст мэлхий
### [Jast mèlxij]

Turtle

## Чоно
### [Čono]

Wolf

## Матар
### [Matar]

Crocodile

## Динозавр
### [Dinozavr]

Dinosaur

## Анааш
### [Anaaš]

Giraffe

## Имж
### [Imž]

Kangaroo

## Гүрвэл
### [Gürvèl]

Lizard

## Бар
### [Bar]

Tiger

## Цоохор тахь
### [Cooxor tax']

Zebra

## Аварга загас
### [Avarga zagas]

**Shark**

## Хавч
### [Xavč]

**Crab**

## Дельфин
### [Del'fin]

**Dolphin**

## Далайн мөгөөрс
### [Dalajn mögöörs]

**Jellyfish**

## Хавч
### [Xavč]

**Lobster**

## Далайн морь
### [Dalajn mor']

**Seahorse**

## Налуу загас
### [Naluu zagas]

**Ray**

## Наймаалж
### [Najmaalž]

**Octopus**

## Эрвээхэй
### [Ěrvèèxèj]

**Butterfly**

## Жоом
### [Žoom]

**Cockroach**

## Аалз
### [Aalz]

**Spider**

## Цох
### [Cox]

**Beetle**

## Тэмээлзгэнэ
### [Tèmèèlzgènè]

**Dragonfly**

## Шоргоолж
### [Šorgoolž]

**Ant**

## Зөгий
### [Zögij]

**Bee**

| ӨДӨР [ÖDÖR] | DAY |
|---|---|

| ДАВАА [DAVAA] | МЯГМАР [MJAGMAR] | ЛХАГВА [LXAGVA] | ПҮРЭВ [PÜRÈV] |
|---|---|---|---|
| MONDAY | TUESDAY | WEDNESDAY | THURSDAY |

| БААСАН [BAASAN] | БЯМБА [BJAMBA] | НЯМ [NJAM] | ДОЛОО ХОНОГ [DOLOO XONOG] |
|---|---|---|---|
| FRIDAY | SATURDAY | SUNDAY | WEEK |

| ЦАГ ХУГАЦАА [CAG XUGACAA] | TIME |
|---|---|

**18**

| ЦАГ [CAG] | МИНУТ [MINUT] |
|---|---|
| HOUR | MINUTE |

| ЖИЛ [ŽIL] | YEAR |
|---|---|

| САР [SAR] | MONTH |
|---|---|

| НЭГДҮГЭЭР САР [NÈGDÜGÈÈR SAR] | ХОЁРДУГААР САР [XOËRDUGAAR SAR] | ГУРАВДУГААР САР [GURAVDUGAAR SAR] | ДӨРӨВДҮГЭЭР САР [DÖRÖVDÜGÈÈR SAR] |
|---|---|---|---|
| JANUARY | FEBRUARY | MARCH | APRIL |

| ТАВДУГААР САР [TAVDUGAAR SAR] | ЗУРГАДУГААР САР [ZURGADUGAAR SAR] | ДОЛДУГААР САР [DOLDUGAAR SAR] | НАЙМДУГААР САР [NAJMDUGAAR SAR] |
|---|---|---|---|
| MAY | JUNE | JULY | AUGUST |

| ЕСДҮГЭЭР САР [ESDÜGÈÈR SAR] | АРАВДУГААР САР [ARAVDUGAAR SAR] | АРВАННЭГДҮГЭЭР САР [ARVANNÈGDÜGÈÈR SAR] | АРВАНХОЁРДУГААР САР [ARVANXOËRDUGAAR SAR] |
|---|---|---|---|
| SEPTEMBER | OCTOBER | NOVEMBER | DECEMBER |

# Өвөл
[Övöl]
**Winter**

# Хавар
[Xavar]
**Spring**

# Намар
[Namar]
**Autumn**

# Зун
[Zun]
**Summer**

# Улирал
[Uliral]
**Season**

# Салхи
[Salxi]
**Wind**

# Бороо
[Boroo]
**Rain**

# Аянга цахилгаан
[Ajanga caxilgaan]
**Thunderstorm**

# Өглөө
[Öglöö]
**Morning**

# Үдээс хойно
[Üdèès xojno]
**Afternoon**

# Шөнө
[Šönö]
**Night**

# Уур амьсгал
[Uur am'sgal]
**Climate**

# Одоо цаг
[Odoo cag]
**Present**

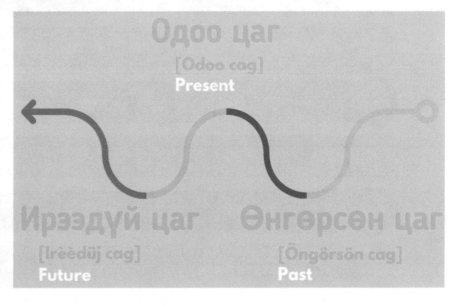

# Ирээдүй цаг
[Irèèdüj cag]
**Future**

# Өнгөрсөн цаг
[Öngörsön cag]
**Past**

# ҮЙЛ ҮГНҮҮД

[üjl ügnüüd]

verbs

| | | |
|---|---|---|
| байх / -тай | [bajx/-taj] | have |
| байх | [bajx] | be |
| хийх | [xijx] | do |
| хэлэх | [xèlèx] | say |
| чадах | [čadax] | can |
| явах | [javax] | go |
| харах | [xarax] | see |
| мэдэх | [mèdèx] | know |
| хүсэх | [xüsèx] | want |
| ирэх | [irèx] | come |
| хэрэгтэй байх | [xèrègtèj bajx] | need |
| ёстой | [ёstoj] | have to |
| итгэх | [itgèx] | believe |
| олох | [olox] | find |
| өгөх | [ögöx] | give |

# ҮЙЛ ҮГНҮҮД

[üjl ügnüüd]

verbs

| | | |
|---|---|---|
| авах | [avax] | take |
| ярих | [jarix] | talk |
| тавих | [tavix] | put |
| санагдах | [sanagdax] | seem |
| орхих | [orxix] | leave |
| үлдэх | [üldèx] | stay |
| бодох | [bodox] | think |
| харах | [xarax] | look |
| хариулах | [xariulax] | answer |
| хүлээх | [xülèèx] | wait |
| амьдрах | [am'drax] | live |
| ойлгох | [ojlgox] | understand |
| орж ирэх | [orž irèx] | come in |
| болох | [bolox] | become |
| эргэж ирэх | [èrgèž irèx] | come back |

# ҮЙЛ ҮГНҮҮД

[üjl ügnüüd]

verbs

| бичих | [bičix] | write |
| дуудах | [duudax] | call |
| унах | [unax] | fall |
| эхлэх | [èxlèx] | start |
| дагах | [dagax] | follow |
| харуулах | [xaruulax] | show |
| инээх | [inèèx] | laugh |
| инээмсэглэх | [inèèmsèglèx] | smile |
| санах | [sanax] | remember |
| тоглох | [toglox] | play |
| идэх | [idèx] | eat |
| унших | [unšix] | read |
| авах | [avax] | get |
| уйлах | [ujlax] | cry |
| тайлбарлах | [tajlbarlax] | explain |

# ҮЙЛ ҮГНҮҮД

[üjl ügnüüd]

verbs

| дуулах | [duulax] | sing |
| хүрэх | [xürèx] | touch |
| үнэрлэх | [ünèrlèx] | smell |
| амьсгалах | [am'sgalax] | breathe |
| сонсох | [sonsox] | hear |
| зурах | [zurax] | paint |
| сурах | [surax] | study |
| тэмдэглэх | [tèmdèglèx] | celebrate |
| сонсох | [sonsox] | choose |
| хайх | [xajx] | search |
| асуух | [asuux] | ask |
| дуртай байх | [durtaj bajx] | enjoy |
| төсөөлөх | [tösöölöx] | imagine |
| уух | [uux] | drink |
| өөрчлөх | [öörčlöx] | change |

**Цагаан толгой**
[Cagaan tolgoj]
Alphabet

**Харандаа**
[Xarandaa]
Pencil

**Хайч**
[Xajč]
Scissors

**Дэвтэр**
[Dèvtèr]
Notebook

**Сурагчийн цүнх**
[Suragčijn cünx]
Schoolbag

**Сурагч**
[Suragč]
Student

**Хичээлийн танхим**
[Xičèèlijn tanxim]
Classroom

**Найзууд**
[Najzuud]
Friends

**Профессор**
[Professor]
Professor

**Математик**
[Matematik]
Mathematics

$$1+3=$$
$$2\times2=$$

**Түүх**
[Tüüx]
History

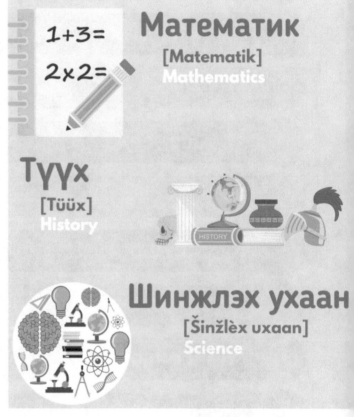

**Шинжлэх ухаан**
[Šinžlèx uxaan]
Science

**Сургууль**
[Surguul']
School

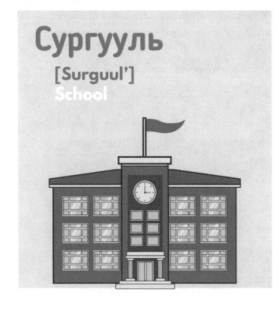

**Уран зураг**
[Uran zurag]
Arts

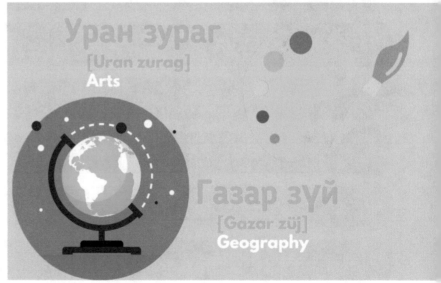

**Газар зүй**
[Gazar züj]
Geography

# Ажил мэргэжил
## [ažil mèrgèžil]

**job**

**сувилагч**
[suvilagč]
NURSE

**фермер**
[fermer]
FARMER

**архитектор**
[arxitektor]
ARCHITECT

**инженер**
[inžener]
ENGINEER

**ажилчин**
[ažilčin]
LABORER

**гал сөнөөгч**
[gal sönöögč]
FIREFIGHTER

**цэцэрлэгч**
[cècèrlègč]
GARDENER

**хуульч**
[xuul'č]
LAWYER

**нисгэгч**
[nisgègč]
PILOT

**жүжигчин**
[žüžigčin]
ACTOR

**шүдний эмч**
[šüdnij èmč]
DENTIST

**механик**
[mexanik]
MECHANIC

**хог ачигч**
[xog ačigč]
DUSTMAN

**нягтлан бодогч**
[njagtlan bodogč]
ACCOUNTANT

**сэтгэл зүйч**
[sètgèl züjč]
PSYCHOLOGIST

**job**

## сэтгүүлч
[sètgüülč]
**JOURNALIST**

## мужаан
[mužaan]
**CARPENTER**

## хөгжимчин
[xögžimčin]
**MUSICIAN**

## сантехникч
[santexnikč]
**PLUMBER**

## тогооч
[togooč]
**COOK**

## зохиолч
[zoxiolč]
**WRITER**

## үсчин
[üsčin]
**HAIRDRESSER**

## нарийн бичиг
[narijn bičig]
**SECRETARY**

## жолооч
[žolooč]
**DRIVER**

## цагдаа
[cagdaa]
**POLICEMAN**

## эмч
[èmč]
**DOCTOR**

## малын эмч
[malyn èmč]
**VETERINARIAN**

## нүдний эмч
[nüdnij èmč]
**OPTICIAN**

## хүүхдийн эмч
[xüüxdijn èmč]
**PEDIATRICIAN**

## зөөгч
[zöögč]
**WAITER**

**ЧАВГА**
[čavga]
PLUM

**ТООР**
[toor]
PEACH

**ИНТООР**
[intoor]
CHERRY

**АЛИМ**
[alim]
APPLE

**УСАН ҮЗЭМ**
[usan üzèm]
GRAPE

**ТАРВАС**
[tarvas]
WATERMELON

**ХАНБОРГОЦОЙ**
[xanborgocoj]
PINEAPPLE

**ГҮЗЭЭЛЗГЭНЭ**
[güzèèlzgènè]
STRAWBERRY

**БӨӨРӨЛЗГӨНӨ**
[bөөrөlzgөnө]
RASPBERRY

**ЛИЙР**
[lijr]
PEAR

**ГАДИЛ**
[gadil]
BANANA

**АМТАТ ГУА**
[amtat gua]
MELON

**НИМБЭГ**
[nimbèg]
LEMON

**ҮХРИЙН НҮД**
[üxrijn nüd]
BLACKBERRY

**ЖҮРЖ**
[žürž]
ORANGE

**МӨӨГ**

[möög]

MUSHROOM

**БРОККОЛИ**

[brokkoli]

BROCCOLI

**БАЙЦАА**

[bajcaa]

CABBAGE

**ХЭРЭЭНИЙ НҮД**

[xèrèènij nüd]

ASPARAGUS

**ӨРГӨСТ ХЭМХ**

[örgöst xèmx]

CUCUMBER

**ЛУУВАН**

[luuvan]

CARROT

**РЕДИСК**

[redisk]

RADISH

**САЛАТНЫ НАВЧ**

[salatny navč]

LETTUCE

**ТӨМС**

[töms]

POTATO

**УЛААН ЛООЛЬ**

[ulaan lool']

TOMATO

**АВОКАДО**

[avokado]

AVOCADO

**ЖУУЦАЙ**

[žuucaj]

LEEK

**ХҮРЭН МАНЖИН**

[xürèn manžin]

BEETROOT

**ХАШ**

[xaš]

EGGPLANT

**АРТИШОК**

[artišok]

ARTICHOKE

**Тайван**
[Tajvan]
**Calm**

**Аз жаргалтай**
[Az žargaltaj]
**Happy**

**Урам хугарсан**
[Uram xugarsan]
**Disappointed**

**Сэтгэл хөдөлсөн**
[Sètgèl xödölsön]
**Excited**

**Айсан**
[Ajsan]
**Frightened**

**Үглээ**
[Üglèè]
**Grumpy**

**Хайртай**
[Xajrtaj]
**In Love**

**Гайхширсан**
[Gajxširsan]
**Surprised**

**Ичимхий**
[Ičimxij]
**Shy**

**Бахархах**
[Baxarxax]
**Proud**

**Ууртай**
[Uurtaj]
**Angry**

**Будилсан**
[Budilsan]
**Confused**

**Ядарсан**
[Jadarsan]
**Tired**

**Сандарсан**
[Sandarsan]
**Nervous**

**Сониуч**
[Soniuč]
**Curious**

**feelings**

| | | |
|---|---|---|
| гайхалтай | [gajxaltaj] | fantastic |
| хачин | [xačin] | weird |
| хэцүү | [xècüü] | hard |
| инээдтэй | [inèèdtèj] | funny |
| хачирхалтай | [xačirxaltaj] | strange |
| амархан | [amarxan] | easy |
| боломжгүй | [bolomžgüj] | impossible |
| залуухан | [zaluuxan] | young |
| зөв | [zöv] | correct |
| чөлөөтэй | [čölöötèj] | free |
| өвчтэй | [övčtèj] | sick |
| адил | [adil] | same |
| ядуу | [jaduu] | poor |
| боломжтой | [bolomžtoj] | possible |
| цэвэр | [cèvèr] | clean |

# Тэмдэг нэрнүүд
[Tèmdèg nèrnüüd]

adjectives

|  | |  |
|---|---|---|
| бохир | [boxir] | dirty |
| энгийн | [èngijn] | simple |
| гунигтай | [gunigtaj] | sad |
| хоосон | [xooson] | empty |
| сайн | [sajn] | good |
| зөөлөн | [zöölön] | soft |
| хуурамч | [xuuramč] | false |
| том | [tom] | big |
| муу | [muu] | bad |
| нухацтай | [nuxactaj] | serious |
| хуучин | [xuučin] | old |
| үнэн | [ünèn] | true |
| сайхан | [sajxan] | beautiful |
| халуун | [xaluun] | hot |
| хүйтэн | [xüjtèn] | cold |

| Mongolian | Pronunciation | English |
|---|---|---|
| үнэтэй | [ünètèj] | expensive |
| тодорхой | [todorxoj] | clear |
| сүүлийн | [süülijn] | last |
| өөр | [öör] | different |
| хүчтэй | [xüčtèj] | strong |
| гоё/сайн | [goë/sajn] | nice |
| өндөр | [öndör] | high |
| хүнлэг | [xünlèg] | human |
| чухал | [čuxal] | important |
| хөөрхөн | [xöörxön] | pretty |
| хөнгөн | [xöngön] | light |
| жижиг | [žižig] | small |
| шинэ | [šinè] | new |
| дүүрэн | [düürèn] | full |
| эхний | [èxnij] | first |

# Өвс
[Övs]
Grass

# Хорхой шавж
[Xorxoj šavž]
Insect

# Цас
[Cas]
Snow

# Уул
[Uul]
Mountain

# Цэцэг
[Cècèg]
Flower

# Агаар
[Agaar]
Air

# Үүл
[Üöl]
Cloud

# Тэнгэр
[Tèngèr]
Sky

# Манан
[Manan]
Fog

# Далай
[Dalaj]
Sea

# Нуур
[Nuur]
Lake

# Далайн эрэг
[Dalajn èrèg]
Beach

# Нар
[Nar]
Sun

# Ой
[Oj]
Forest

# Мод
[Mod]
Tree

СОНИН

[sonin]

NEWSPAPER

КИНО ТЕАТР

[kino teatr]

CINEMA

ЗУРАГТ

[zuragt]

TELEVISION

НОМ

[nom]

BOOK

УРАН БАРИМАЛ

[uran barimal]

SCULPTURE

ГЭРЭЛ ЗУРАГ

[gèrèl zurag]

PHOTOGRAPHY

ДУУ ХӨГЖИМ

[duu xögžim]

MUSIC

ТОГЛОЛТ

[toglolt]

CONCERT

КИНО

[kino]

MOVIE

КОМПЬЮТЕР

[komp'juter]

COMPUTER

ТОЛЬ БИЧИГ

[tol' bičig]

DICTIONARY

УРАН ЗУРАГ

[uran zurag]

PAINTING

МУЗЕЙ

[muzej]

MUSEUM

ДУУРЬ

[duur']

OPERA

ТЕАТР

[teatr]

THEATER

# ӨНГӨНҮҮД
## [öngönüüd]

## colors

| | | | |
|---|---|---|---|
| **ЦЭНХЭР** [cènxèr] | blue | **хар** [xar] | black |
| **НИЛ ЯГААН** [nil jagaan] | purple | **цагаан** [cagaan] | white |
| **ЯГААН** [jagaan] | pink | **бор** [bor] | brown |
| **улаан** [ulaan] | red | **алтлаг** [altlag] | gold |
| **улбар шар** [ulbar šar] | orange | **саарал** [saaral] | gray |
| **шар** [šar] | yellow | **мөнгөлөг** [möngölög] | silver |
| **НОГООН** [nogoon] | green | **СОЛОНГО** [solongo] | rainbow |

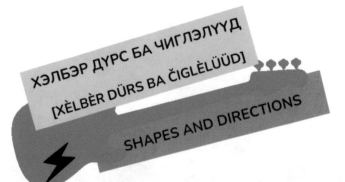

ХЭЛБЭР ДУРС БА ЧИГЛЭЛҮҮД

[XÈLBÈR DÜRS BA ČIGLÈLÜÜD]

SHAPES AND DIRECTIONS

|  | |  |
|---|---|---|
| урд талд | [urd tald] | in front of |
| ард | [ard] | behind |
| зүүн | [züün] | left |
| баруун | [baruun] | right |
| дунд | [dund] | middle |
| дөрвөлжин | [dörvölžin] | square |
| дугуй | [duguj] | circle |
| тэгш өнцөгт | [tègš öncögt] | rectangle |
| шоо | [šoo] | cube |
| ромбо | [rombo] | diamond |
| шугам | [šugam] | line |
| баруун | [baruun] | west |
| зүүн | [züün] | east |
| хойно | [xojno] | north |
| өмнө | [ömnö] | south |

## ГАЛ ТОГОО
### [GAL TOGOO]
KITCHEN

## ХААЛГА
### [XAALGA]
DOOR

## ЗОЧНЫ ӨРӨӨ
### [ZOČNY ÖRÖÖ]
DINING ROOM

## АРИУН ЦЭВРИЙН ӨРӨӨ
### [ARIUN CÈVRIJN ÖRÖÖ]
BATHROOM

## ЦОНХ
### [CONX]
WINDOW

## ШАТ
### [ŠAT]
STAIRS

## ДЭЭВРИЙН ХӨНДИЙ
### [DÈÈVRIJN XÖNDIJ]
ATTIC

## КОРИДОР
### [KORIDOR]
HALL

## АЖЛЫН ӨРӨӨ
### [AŽLYN ÖRÖÖ]
OFFICE

## ТАГТ
### [TAGT]
BALCONY

## ХОНГИЛ
### [XONGIL]
BASEMENT
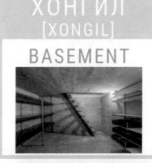

## ХӨРШ
### [XÖRŠ]
NEIGHBOR

## ЦЭЦЭРЛЭГ
### [CÈCÈRLÈG]
GARDEN

## УНТЛАГЫН ӨРӨӨ
### [UNTLAGYN ÖRÖÖ]
BEDROOM

# ГЭР
## [GÈR]

# HOME

38

| ЦАХИЛГААН ЗУУХ [CAXILGAAN ZUUX] | ПААР [PAAR] | БУЙДАН [BUJDAN] | ХӨРГӨГЧ [XÖRGÖGČ] |
|---|---|---|---|
| OVEN | RADIATOR | SOFA | FRIDGE |

| ШИРЭЭНИЙ ГЭРЭЛ [ŠIRÈÈNIJ GÈRÈL] | УГААЛТУУР [UGAALTUUR] | ГАР УТАС [GAR UTAS] | ШИЛЭН АЯГА [ŠILÈN AJAGA] |
|---|---|---|---|
| LAMP | SINK | TELEPHONE | GLASS |

| ТАВАГ [TAVAG] | ТОЛЬ [TOL'] | ЦАГ [CAG] | САНДАЛ [SANDAL] |
|---|---|---|---|
| PLATE | MIRROR | CLOCK | CHAIR |

| ОР [OR] | ШИРЭЭ [ŠIRÈÈ] |
|---|---|
| BED | TABLE |

## ХАНА
### [XANA]
WALL

## ДЭЭВЭР
### [ДЭЭВЭР]
ROOF

## ХӨЛДӨӨГЧ
### [XÖLDÖÖGČ]
FREEZER

## АЯГАНЫ ШУУГЭЭ
### [AJAGANY ŠÜÜGÈÈ]
CUPBOARD

## УРГАМАЛ
### [URGAMAL]
PLANT

## ЗАДГАЙ ЗУУХ
### [ZADGAJ ZUUX]
FIREPLACE

## ТООС СОРОГЧ
### [TOOS SOROGČ]
VACUUM CLEANER

## ЦОРГО
### [CORGO]
TAP

## АЯГА ТАВАГ УГААГЧ
### [AJAGA TAVAG UGAAGČ]
DISHWASHER

## БОГИНО ДОЛГИОНЫ ЗУУХ
### [BOGINO DOLGIONY ZUUX]
MICROWAVE

## ХИВС
### [XIVS]
CARPET

## ХОНХ
### [XONX]
DOORBELL

## ЦОНХНЫ ХААЛТ
### [CONXNY XAALT]
SHUTTER

## ТҮЛХҮҮР
### [TÜLXÜÜR]
KEY

## АЛЧУУР
[ALČUUR]

TOWEL

## ОР ДЭРНИЙ ДААВУУ
[OR DÈRNIJ DAAVUU]

BED SHEET

## САВАН
[SAVAN]

SOAP

## САМ
[SAM]

COMB

## ХӨШИГ
[XÖŠIG]

CURTAIN

## АЯГА
[AJAGA]

CUP

## ШУРШУУР
[ŠÜRŠÜÜR]

SHOWER

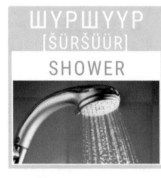

## ГЭРЛИЙН ЧИЙДЭН
[GÈRLIJN ČIJDÈN]

LIGHTBULB

## СЭРЭЭ
[SÈRÈÈ]

FORK

## ХАЛБАГА
[XALBAGA]

SPOON

## ХУТГА
[XUTGA]

KNIFE

## БАНН
[BANN]

BATHTUB

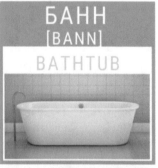

## УСНЫ САВ
[USNY SAV]

BOTTLE

## ХОГИЙН САВ
[XOGIJN SAV]

GARBAGE CAN

# Угтвар үгнүүд
## [Ugtvar ügnüüd]

**prepositions**

|  |  |  |
|-----------|---------------|---------|
| **-д** | [-d] | for |
| **дараа** | [daraa] | after |
| **θмнθ** | [ömnö] | before |
| **хамт** | [xamt] | with |
| **тухай** | [tuxaj] | about |
| **эсрэг** | [èsrèg] | against |
| **дотор** | [dotor] | in |
| **-гүй** | [-güj] | without |
| **хойш** | [xojš] | since |
| **дэргэд** | [dèrgèd] | around |
| **дээр** | [dèèr] | on |
| **адил** | [adil] | like |
| **турш** | [turš] | during |
| **хооронд** | [xoorond] | between |
| **-аас** | [-aas] | from |

# Хүн
## [Xün]

# Human

---

## бие
### [bie]
**body**

## толгой
### [tolgoj]
**head**

## гар
### [gar]
**hand**

---

## үс
### [üs]
**hair**

## нүүр
### [nüür]
**face**

## хуруу
### [xuruu]
**finger**

---

## чих
### [čix]
**ear**

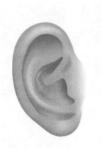

## нүд
### [nüd]
**eyes**

## хумс
### [xums]
**nail**

---

## хамар
### [xamar]
**nose**

## ам
### [am]
**mouth**

## хөл
### [xöl]
**leg**

---

## шүд
### [šüd]
**tooth**

## уруул
### [uruul]
**lips**

## хөлийн тавхай
### [xölijn tavxaj]
**foot**

# Хүн
## [Xün]

# Human

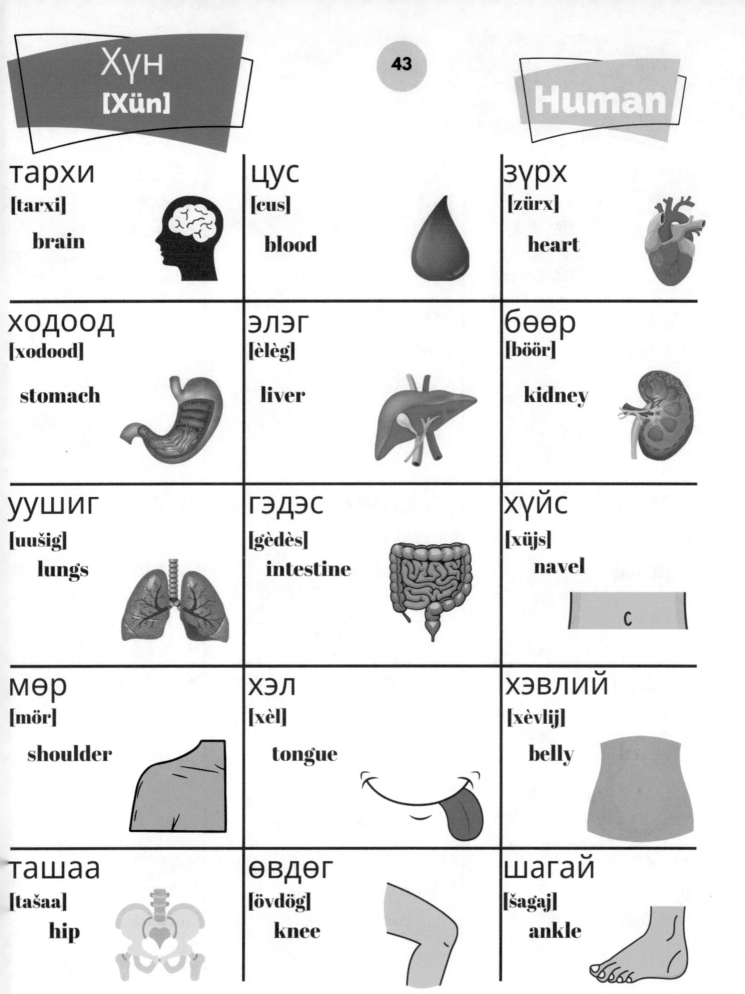

**тархи**
[tarxi]
brain

**цус**
[cus]
blood

**зүрх**
[zürx]
heart

**ходоод**
[xodood]
stomach

**элэг**
[èlèg]
liver

**бөөр**
[böör]
kidney

**уушиг**
[uušig]
lungs

**гэдэс**
[gèdès]
intestine

**хүйс**
[xüjs]
navel

**мөр**
[mör]
shoulder

**хэл**
[xèl]
tongue

**хэвлий**
[xèvlij]
belly

**ташаа**
[tašaa]
hip

**өвдөг**
[övdög]
knee

**шагай**
[šagaj]
ankle

# Хүн
## [Xün]

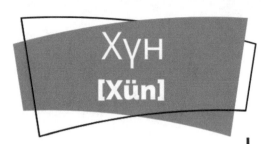

# Human

| | | |
|---|---|---|
| **арьс** [ar's] skin  | **яс** [jas] bone  | **гавал** [gaval] skull  |
| **хүзүү** [xüzüü] neck  | **бугуй** [buguj] wrist  | **хөмсөг** [xömsög] eyebrow  |
| **хоолой** [xooloj] throat  | **давхраа** [davxraa] eyelid  | **эрүү** [èrüü] chin  |
| **сахал** [saxal] beard  | **жирвэгэр сахал** [žirvègèr saxal] mustache  | **булчин** [bulčin] muscle  |
| **тохой** [toxoj] elbow  | **хөлийн эрхий хуруу** [xölijn èrxij xuruu] toe  | **хацар** [xacar] cheek  |

# Цаг хугацаа
## [Cag xugacaa]

time

| Монгол | [Transliteration] | English |
|---|---|---|
| өчигдөр | [öčigdör] | yesterday |
| өнөөдөр | [önöödör] | today |
| маргааш | [margaaš] | tomorrow |
| одоо | [odoo] | now |
| удахгүй | [udaxgüj] | soon |
| хожуу | [xožuu] | late |
| энд | [ènd] | here |
| зай | [zaj] | distance |
| нар мандах | [nar mandax] | sunrise |
| үд дунд | [üd dund] | noon |
| орой | [oroj] | evening |
| шөнө дунд | [šönö dund] | midnight |
| арван жил | [arvan žil] | decade |
| зуун | [zuun] | century |
| мянган жил | [mjangan žil] | millennium |

# Европ
**[Evrop]**

Europe

# Африк
**[Afrik]**

Africa

# Ази
**[Azi]**

Asia

# Америк
**[Amerik]**

America

# Англи
**[Angli]**

England

# Герман
**[German]**

Germany

# Франц
**[Franc]**

France

# Испани
**[Ispani]**

Spain

# Итали
**[Itali]**

Italy

Америкийн Нэгдсэн улс
**[Amerikijn Nègdsèn uls ]**

United States

# Бразил
**[Brazil]**

Brazil

# Япон
**[Japon]**
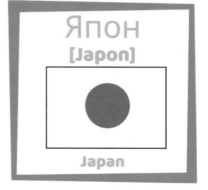
Japan

# Хятад
**[Xjatad]**

China

# Энэтхэг
**[Ènètxèg]**

India

# Орос
**[Oros]**

Russia

# Мексик
**[Meksik]**

**Mexico**

# Египт
**[Egipt]**

**Egypt**

# Турк
**[Turk]**

**Turkey**

# Нигер
**[Niger]**

**Nigeria**

# Тайланд
**[Tajland]**

**Thailand**

# Өмнөд Солонгос
**[Ömnöd Solongos]**

**South Korea**

# Колумб
**[Kolumb]**

**Colombia**

# Аргентин
**[Argentin]**

**Argentina**

# Алжир
**[Alžir]**

**Algeria**

# Польш
**[Pol'š]**

**Poland**

# Саудын Араб
**[Saudyn Arab]**

**Saudi Arabia**

# Камерун
**[Kamerun]**

**Cameroon**

# Нидерланд
**[Niderland]**

**Netherlands**

# Швейцар
**[Švejcar]**

**Switzerland**

# Швед
**[Šved]**

**Sweden**

Улс орон

[uls oron]

country

## Грек
**[Grek]**

Greece

## Бельги
**[Bel'gi]**

Belgium

## Ирланд
**[Irland]**

Ireland

## Норвеги
**[Norvegi]**

Norway

## Австрали
**[Avstrali]**

Australia

## Дани
**[Dani]**

Denmark

## Австри
**[Avstri]**

Austria

## Финлянд
**[Finljand]**

Finland

## Португаль
**[Portugal']**

Portugal

## Өмнөд Африк
**[Ömnöd Afrik]**

South Africa

## Индонези
**[Indonezi]**

Indonesia

## Танзани
**[Tanzani]**

Tanzania

## Украин
**[Ukrain]**

Ukraine

## Перу
**[Peru]**

Peru

## Чили
**[Čili]**

Chile

## Европ
[Evrop]

European

## Америк
[Amerik]

American

## Англи
[Angli]

English

## Франц
[Franc]

French

## Испани
[Ispani]

Spanish

## Итали
[Itali]

Italien

## Герман
[German]

German

## Африк
[Afrik]

African

## Ази
[Azi]

Asian

## Орос
[Oros]

Russian

## Хятад
[Xjatad]

Chinese

## Канад
[Kanad]

Canadian

## Энэтхэг
[Ènètxèg]

Indian

## Бразил
[Brazil]

Brazilian

## Мексик
[Meksik]

Mexican

## Өмд
[Ömd]
**Pants**

## Цамц
[Camc]
**Shirt**

## Зангиа
[Zangia]
**Tie**

## Оймс
[Ojms]
**Socks**

## Хүрэм
[Xürèm]
**Jacket**

## Нүдний шил
[Nüdnij šil]
**Glasses**

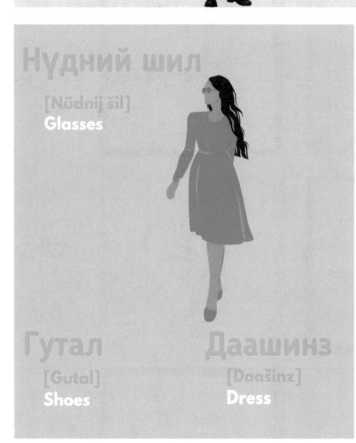

## Гутал
[Gutal]
**Shoes**

## Даашинз
[Daašinz]
**Dress**

## Бүс
[Büs]
**Belt**

## Малгай
[Malgaj]
**Hat**

## Хэтэвч
[Xètèvč]
**Wallet**

## Шүхэр
[Šüxèr]
**Umbrella**

## Дугуй малгай
[Duguj malgaj]
**Beanie**

## Ороолт
[Oroolt]
**Scarf**

## Бээлий
[Bèèlij]
**Gloves**

# Гоёл чимэглэл

[goël čimèglèl]

## accessories

### бугуйвч
[bugujvč]
**BRACELET**

### бугуйн цаг
[bugujn cag]
**WATCH**

### үнэт эдлэл
[ünèt èdlèl]
**JEWELRY**

### бөгж
[bögž]
**RING**

### ээмэг
[èèmèg]
**EARRINGS**

### нусны алчуур
[nusny alčuur]
**HANDKERCHIEF**

### унтлагын хувцас
[untlagyn xuvcas]
**PAJAMAS**

### сандаал
[sandaal]
**SANDALS**

### гутал
[gutal]
**BOOTS**

### гутлын үдээс
[gutlyn üdèès]
**SHOELACE**

### хүзүүний зүүлт
[xüzüünij züült]
**NECKLACE**

### шаахай
[šaaxaj]
**SLIPPERS**

### энгэсэг
[èngèsèg]
**MAKEUP**

### гар цүнх
[gar cünx]
**HANDBAG**

### халаас
[xalaas]
**POCKET**

# Орчлон ертөнц
[Orčlon ertönc]
**Universe**

# Галактик
[Galaktik]
**Galaxy**

# Сүүлт од
[Süült od]
**Comet**

# Тэнгэрийн заадал
[Tèngèrijn zaadal]
**Milky Way**

# Сансар
[Sansar]
**Space**

# Жижиг гараг
[Žižig garag]
**Asteroid**

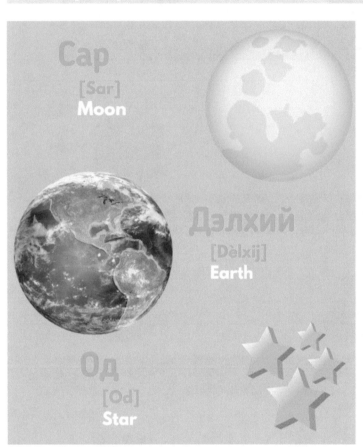

# Сар
[Sar]
**Moon**

# Дэлхий
[Dèlxij]
**Earth**

# Од
[Od]
**Star**

# Цаг хугацаа
[Cag xugacaa]
**Time**

# Гэрэл
[Gèrèl]
**Light**

# Гараг
[Garag]
**Planet**

# Сансрын нисгэгч
[Sansryn nisgègč]
**Astronaut**

# Пуужин
[Puužin]
**Rocket**

# Хиймэл дагуул
[Xijmèl daguul]
**Satellite**

# Үнэ
[Ünè]
Price

# Мөнгө
[Möngö]
Money

# Төлөх
[Tölöx]
To pay

# Үйлчлүүлэгч
[Üjlčlüülègč]
Client

# Бэлэг
[Bèlèg]
Gift

# Цахим
[Caxim]
Online

# Банк
[Bank]
Bank

# Номын дэлгүүр
[Nomyn dèlgüür]
Bookstore

# Эмийн сан
[Èmijn san]
Pharmacy

# Дэлгүүр
[Dèlgüür]
Store

# Ресторан
[Restoran]
Restaurant

# Үдэшлэг
[Üdèšlèg]
Party

# Хурим
[Xurim]
Wedding

# Төрөлт
[Törölt]
Birth

# Төрсөн өдөр
[Törsön ödör]
Birthday

# дайвар үгнүүд
## [dajvar ügnüüd]

adverbs

| | | |
|---|---|---|
| **үргэлж** | [ürgèlž] | always |
| **өөр газар** | [öör gazar] | elsewhere |
| **ойролцоогоор** | [ojrolcoogoor] | approximately |
| **хаа сайгүй** | [xaa sajgüj] | everywhere |
| **хаа нэгтээ** | [xaa nègtèè] | somewhere |
| **хаана ч** | [xaana č] | anywhere |
| **хаана ч үгүй** | [xaana č ügüj] | nowhere |
| **дотор** | [dotor] | inside |
| **гадна** | [gadna] | outside |
| **иймээс** | [ijmèès] | thus |
| **дэргэд** | [dèrgèd] | near |
| **дээр** | [dèèr] | above |
| **аажмаар** | [aažmaar] | slowly |
| **хурдан** | [xurdan] | quickly |
| **үнэхээр** | [ünèxèèr] | really |

# дайвар үгнүүд [dajvar ügnüüd] adverbs

| | | |
|---|---|---|
| зүгээр л | [zügèèr l] | simply |
| үнэнээсээ | [ünènèèsèè] | seriously |
| азаар | [azaar] | fortunately |
| заримдаа | [zarimdaa] | sometimes |
| ховорхон | [xovorxon] | rarely |
| хангалттай | [xangalttaj] | enough |
| юуны өмнө | [juuny ömnö] | firstly |
| өмнө | [ömnö] | before |
| дараа | [daraa] | after |
| гэхдээ | [gèxdèè] | however |
| хэзээ ч | [xèzèè č] | never |
| саяхан | [sajaxan] | recently |
| дараа нь | [daraa n'] | then |
| дандаа | [dandaa] | often |
| ихэвчлэн | [ixèvčlèn] | usually |

# дайвар үгнүүд
## [dajvar ügnüüd]

## adverbs

|  |  |  |
|---|---|---|
| **илүү** | [ilüü] | better |
| **нэлээд** | [nèlèèd] | well |
| **маш** | [maš] | a lot |
| **чухамдаа** | [čuxamdaa] | rather |
| **нэлээд** | [nèlèèd] | quite |
| **тиймээс** | [tijmèès] | so |
| **бас** | [bas] | too |
| **бага зэрэг** | [baga zèrèg] | little |
| **хамаагүй** | [xamaagüj] | far |
| **маш/үнэхээр** | [maš/ünèxèèr] | very |
| **бараг** | [barag] | almost |
| **аль хэдийн** | [al' xèdijn] | already |
| **хойш** | [xojš] | since |
| **гэнэт** | [gènèt] | suddenly |
| **яриангүй** | [jariangüj] | indeed |

### Нялх хүүхэд
[Njalx xüüxèd]
**Baby**

### Хүүхэд
[Xüüxèd]
**Child**

### Хүү
[Xüü]
**Boy**

### Охин
[Oxin]
**Girl**

### Өсвөр үе
[Ösvör üe]
**Teenager**

### Эмэгтэй
[Èmègtèj]
**Woman**

### Эрэгтэй
[Èrègtèj]
**Man**

### Насанд хүрэгч
[Nasand xürègč]
**Adult**

### Найз
[Najz]
**Friend**

### Үеэл
[Üeèl]
**Cousin**

### Ажлын хамтрагч
[Ažlyn xamtragč]
**Colleague**

### Хайр
[Xajr]
**Love**

### Нөхөрлөл
[Nöxörlöl]
**Friendship**

### Аз жаргал
[Az žargal]
**Happiness**

### Баяр баясал
[Bajar bajasal]
**Joy**

# спорт
## [sport]

# sport

**баг**
[bag]
**TEAM**

**тоглогч**
[toglogč]
**PLAYER**

**стадион**
[stadion]
**STADIUM**

**хөл бөмбөг**
[xöl bömbög]
**FOOTBALL/SOCCER**

**шүүгч**
[šüügč]
**REFEREE**

**бөмбөг**
[bömbög]
**BALL**

**өмсгөл**
[ömsgöl]
**JERSEY**

**дасгалжуулалт**
[dasgalžuulalt]
**TRAINING**

**зэрэглэл**
[zèrèglèl]
**RANKING**

**морь унах**
[mor' unax]
**HORSE RIDING**

**дугуй унах**
[duguj unax]
**CYCLING**

**усан сэлэлт**
[usan sèlèlt]
**SWIMMING**

**дасгалжуулагч**
[dasgalžuulagč]
**COACH**

**бэртэл**
[bèrtèl]
**INJURY**

**хөнгөн атлетик**
[xöngön atletik]
**TRACK AND FIELD**

# Засгийн газар
[Zasgijn gazar]
**Government**

# Ерөнхийлөгч
[Erönxijlögč]
**President**

# Дэлхий
[Dèlxij]
**World**

# Улс төр
[Uls tör]
**Politics**

# Хотын дарга
[Xotyn darga]
**Mayor**

# Улс орон
[Uls oron]
**Country**

# Хүмүүс
[Xümüüs]
**People**

# Тив
[Tiv]
**Continent**

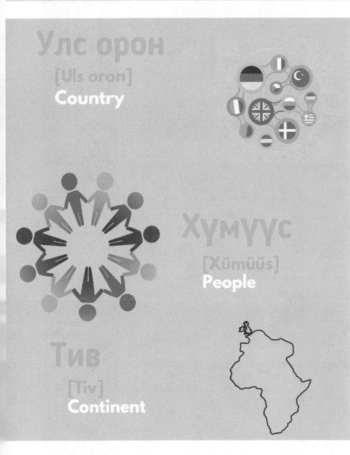

# Хот
[Xot]
**City**

# Жижиг хот
[Žižig xot]
**Town**

# Цэцэрлэг
[Cècèrlèg]
**Park**

# Компани
[Kompani]
**Company**

# Арал
[Aral]
**Island**

# Элсэн цөл
[Èlsèn cöl]
**Desert**

# Эмнэлэг
[Èmnèlèg]
**Hospital**

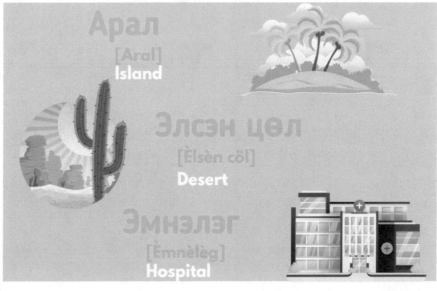

Нийгмийн
сүлжээ
**[Nijgmijn sülžèè]**

Social network

Хэрэглэгч
**[Xèrèglègč]**

User

Нийтлэх
**[Nijtlèx]**

Publish

Хуваалцах
**[Xuvaalcax]**

Share

Контент
**[Kontent]**

Content

Бүртгүүлэх
**[Bürtgüülèx]**

Subscribe

Мэдээ
**[Mèdèè]**

News

Сурталчилгаа
**[Surtalčilgaa]**

Advertising

Дагах
**[Dagax]**

Follow

Аккаунт
**[Akkaunt]**

Account

Суваг
**[Suvag]**

Channel

Судалгаа
**[Sudalgaa]**

Research

Коммент
**[Komment]**

Comment

Чатлах
**[Čatlax]**

Chat

Холбоос
**[Xolboos]**

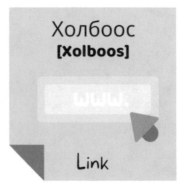

Link

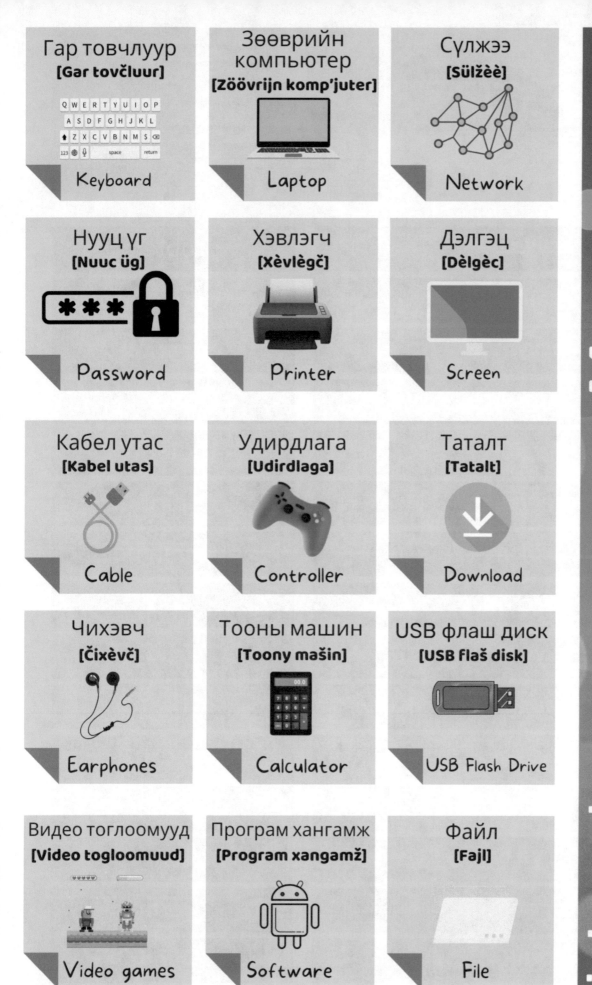

Гар товчлуур
**[Gar tovčluur]**

Keyboard

Зөөврийн компьютер
**[Zöövrijn komp'juter]**

Laptop

Сүлжээ
**[Sülžèè]**

Network

Нууц үг
**[Nuuc üg]**

Password

Хэвлэгч
**[Xèvlègč]**

Printer

Дэлгэц
**[Dèlgèc]**

Screen

Кабел утас
**[Kabel utas]**

Cable

Удирдлага
**[Udirdlaga]**

Controller

Таталт
**[Tatalt]**

Download

Чихэвч
**[Čixèvč]**

Earphones

Тооны машин
**[Toony mašin]**

Calculator

USB флаш диск
**[USB flaš disk]**

USB Flash Drive

Видео тоглоомууд
**[Video togloomuud]**

Video games

Програм хангамж
**[Program xangamž]**

Software

Файл
**[Fajl]**

File

| Mongolian | Pronunciation | English |
|---|---|---|
| асуудал | [asuudal] | problem |
| санаа | [sanaa] | idea |
| асуулт | [asuult] | question |
| хариулт | [xariult] | answer |
| бодол | [bodol] | thought |
| мөн чанар | [mön čanar] | spirit |
| эхлэл | [èxlèl] | beginning |
| төгсгөл | [tögsgöl] | end |
| хууль | [xuul'] | law |
| амьдрал | [am'dral] | life |
| үхэл | [üxèl] | death |
| эв найрамдал | [èv najramdal] | peace |
| чимээгүй байдал | [čimèègüj bajdal] | silence |
| мөрөөдөл | [möröödöl] | dream |
| жин | [žin] | weight |

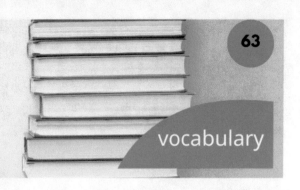
|  |  |  |
|---|---|---|
| үзэл бодол | [üzèl bodol] | opinion |
| зүйл | [züjl] | thing |
| алдаа | [aldaa] | mistake |
| өлсгөлөн | [ölsgölön] | hunger |
| цангаа | [cangaa] | thirst |
| сонголт | [songolt] | choice |
| хүч чадал | [xüč čadal] | strength |
| зураг | [zurag] | picture |
| робот | [robot] | robot |
| худал хуурмаг | [xudal xuurmag] | lie |
| үнэн | [ünèn] | truth |
| дуу чимээ | [duu čimèè] | noise |
| юу ч биш | [juu č biš] | nothing |
| бүх зүйл | [büx züjl] | everything |
| хагас | [xagas] | half |

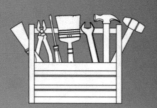

| сүх | өрөм | цавуу |
|-----|------|-------|
| [süx] | [öröm] | [cavuu] |
| **AXE** | **DRILL** | **GLUE** |

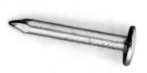

| алх | шат | хадаас |
|-----|-----|--------|
| [alx] | [šat] | [xadaas] |
| **HAMMER** | **LADDER** | **NAIL** |

| халив | тармуур | хадуур |
|-------|---------|--------|
| [xaliv] | [tarmuur] | [xaduur] |
| **SCREWDRIVER** | **RAKE** | **MOWER** |

| хөрөө | картон хайрцаг | түрдэг тэрэг |
|-------|---------------|-------------|
| [xöröö] | [karton xajrcag] | [türdèg tèrèg] |
| **SAW** | **CARDBOARD** | **WHEELBARROW** |

| усалгааны сав | шураг | хүрз |
|---------------|-------|------|
| [usalgaany sav] | [šurag] | [xürz] |
| **WATERING CAN** | **SCREW** | **SHOVEL** |

# үгсийн сан
[ügsijn san]

vocabulary

| Монгол | Галиглал | English |
|---|---|---|
| **харшил** | [xaršil] | allergy |
| **ханиад** | [xaniad] | flu |
| **амралт** | [amralt] | rest |
| **эм** | [èm] | medication |
| **вакцин** | [vakcin] | vaccine |
| **антибиотик** | [antibiotik] | antibiotic |
| **халууралт** | [xaluuralt] | fever |
| **эмчилгээ** | [èmčilgèè] | heal |
| **эрүүл мэнд** | [èrüül mènd] | health |
| **халдвар** | [xaldvar] | infection |
| **шинж тэмдэг** | [šinž tèmdèg] | symptom |
| **халдварладаг** | [xaldvarladag] | contagious |
| **өвчин** | [övčin] | sickness |
| **өвдөлт** | [övdölt] | pain |
| **ханиалга** | [xanialga] | cough |

Атом
**[Atom]**
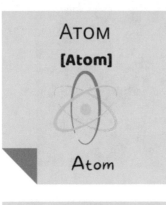
Atom

Нян бактери
**[Njan bakteri]**
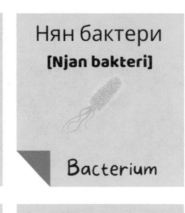
Bacterium

Эд эс
**[Èd ès]**
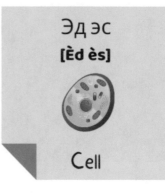
Cell

Хими
**[Ximi]**
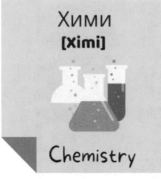
Chemistry

Биологи
**[Biologi]**
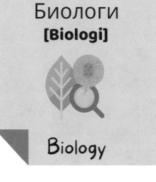
Biology

Микроскоп
**[Mikroskop]**

Microscope

Молекул
**[Molekul]**
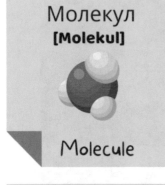
Molecule

Тооцоолол
**[Toocoolol]**
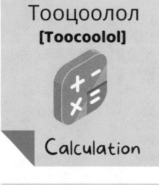
Calculation

Үр дүн
**[Ür dün]**

Result

Нийлбэр
**[Nijlbèr]**

Addition

Хасалт
**[Xasalt]**
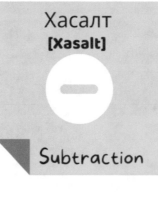
Subtraction

Хуваалт
**[Xuvaalt]**

Division

Үржүүлэлт
**[Üržüülèlt]**

Multiplication

Хаалт
**[Xaalt]**

Parenthesis

Хувь хэмжээ
**[Xuv' xèmžèè]**

Percentage

**их сургууль**

[ix surguul']

UNIVERSITY

**үйлдвэр**

[üjldvèr]

FACTORY

**барилга**

[barilga]

BUILDING

**шорон**

[šoron]

JAIL

**хотын захиргаа**

[xotyn zaxirgaa]

TOWN HALL

**гүүр**

[güür]

BRIDGE

**цамхаг**

[camxag]

CASTLE

**оршуулга**

[oršuulga]

CEMETERY

**усан оргилуур**

[usan orgiluur]

FOUNTAIN

**нүхэн гарц**

[nüxèn garc]

TUNNEL

**амьтны хүрээлэн**

[am'tny xürèèlèn]

ZOO

**шүүх**

[šüüx]

COURT

**цирк**

[cirk]

CIRCUS

**казино**

[kazino]

CASINO

**лаборатори**

[laboratori]

LABORATORY

### Хөвөн
**[Xövön]**

**Cotton**

### Мод
**[Mod]**

**Wood**

### Тоосго
**[Toosgo]**

**Brick**

### Бетон
**[Beton]**

**Concrete**

### Ноос
**[Noos]**

**Wool**

### Арьс
**[Ar's]**

**Leather**

### Металл
**[Metall]**

**Metal**

### Гантиг
**[Gantig]**

**Marble**

### Ган
**[Gan]**
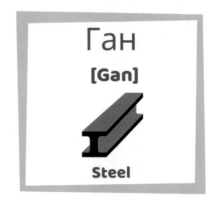
**Steel**

### Шаазан
**[Šaazan]**

**Porcelain**

### Шавар
**[Šavar]**

**Clay**

### Хуванцар
**[Xuvancar]**

**Plastic**

### Резин
**[Rezin]**

**Rubber**

### Цаас
**[Caas]**

**Paper**

### Элс
**[Èls]**
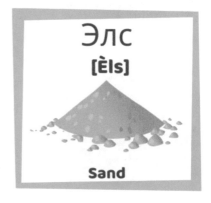
**Sand**

# Газар дэлхий
## [Gazar dèlxij]

| | | |
|---|---|---|
| **газар хөдлөлт** [gazar xödlölt] earthquake  | **гал** [gal] fire  | **хээр тал** [xèèr tal] field  |
| **цасан нуранги** [casan nurangi] avalanche  | **хар салхи** [xar salxi] tornado  | **хадан цохио** [xadan coxio] cliff  |
| **далай** [dalaj] ocean  | **галт уул** [galt uul] volcano  | **элсэн манхан** [èlsèn manxan] dune 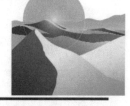 |
| **давалгаа** [davalgaa] wave  | **толгод** [tolgod] hill 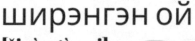 | **мөсөн гол** [mösön gol] glacier |
| **ширэнгэн ой** [širèngèn oj] jungle  | **хөндий** [xöndij] valley  | **агуй** [aguj] cave  |

**найрал хөгжим**
[najral xögžim]
ORCHESTRA

**дуу**
[duu]
SONG

**хөгжимчин**
[xögžimčin]
MUSICIAN

**гитар**
[gitar]
GUITAR

**дуучин**
[duučin]
SINGER

**төгөлдөр хуур**
[tögöldör xuur]
PIANO

**бөмбөр**
[bömbör]
DRUMS

**хийл**
[xijl]
VIOLIN

**бүрээ**
[bürèè]
TRUMPET

**дууны үг**
[duuny üg]
LYRICS

**үзэгч**
[üzègč]
AUDIENCE

**дуу хоолой**
[duu xooloj]
VOICE

**микрофон**
[mikrofon]
MICROPHONE

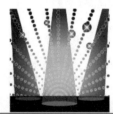

**тайз**
[tajz]
STAGE

**хэмжээ**
[xèmžèè]
VOLUME

# Хаяг
[Xajag]
Address

# Дугтуй
[Dugtuj]
Envelope

# Шуудангийн хайрцаг
[Šuudangijn xajrcag]
Mailbox

# Захидал
[Zaxidal]
Mail

# Шуудангийн марк
[Šuudangijn mark]
Stamp

# Нэхэмжлэх
[Nèxèmžlèx]
Bill

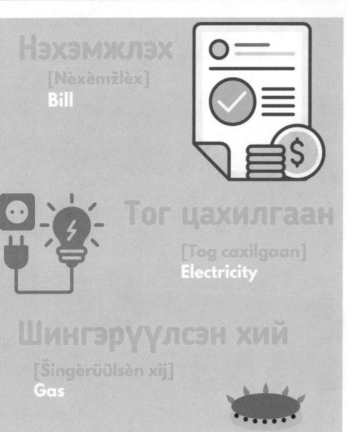

# Тог цахилгаан
[Tog caxilgaan]
Electricity

# Шингэрүүлсэн хий
[Šingèrüülsèn xij]
Gas

# Цалин хөлс
[Calin xöls]
Salary

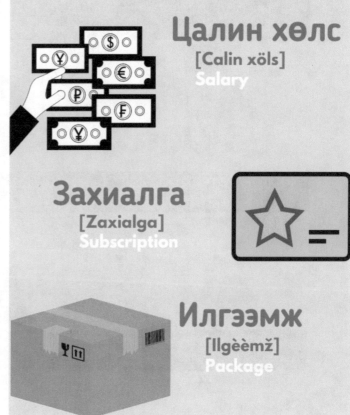

# Захиалга
[Zaxialga]
Subscription

# Илгээмж
[Ilgèèmž]
Package

# Шууданч
[Šuudanč]
Postman

# Илгээх
[Ilgèèx]
Send

# Худалдаж авах
[Xudaldaž avax]
Buy

# Зарах
[Zarax]
Sell

### дахин боловсруулах
[daxin bolovsruulax]
**RECYCLE**

### хүрээлэн буй орчин
[xürèèlèn buj orčin ]
**ENVIRONMENT**

### бохирдол
[boxirdol]
**POLLUTION**

### хортон устгах бодис
[xorton ustgax bodis]
**PESTICIDES**

### органик
[organik]
**ORGANIC**

### цагаан хоолтон
[cagaan xoolton]
**VEGETARIAN**

### эрчим хүч
[èrčim xüč]
**ENERGY**

### нүүрс
[nüürs]
**COAL**

### бензин
[benzin]
**GASOLINE**

### цөмийн
[cömijn]
**NUCLEAR**

### экосистем
[èkosistem]
**ECOSYSTEM**

### амьтны аймаг
[am'tny ajmag]
**FAUNA**

### ургамлын аймаг
[urgamlyn ajmag]
**FLORA**

### температур
[temperatur]
**TEMPERATURE**

### хойд туйл
[xojd tujl]
**ARCTIC**

19201068R00042